Hilary Duff

Hilary Duff

by Terri Dougherty

LUCENT BOOKS

An imprint of Thomson Gale, a part of The Thomson Corporation

THOMSON

━━━━━★━━━━━ ™

GALE

Detroit • New York • San Francisco • New Haven, Conn. • Waterville, Maine • London

For more information, contact:
Lucent Books
27500 Drake Rd.
Farmington Hills, MI 48331-3535
Or you can visit our Internet site at http://www.gale.com

LIBRARY OF CONGRESS CATALOGING-IN-PUBLICATION DATA.

Dougherty, Terri.
  Hilary Duff / by Terri Dougherty.
    p. cm. — (People in the news)
  Includes bibliographical references and index.
  ISBN-13: 978-1-4205-0012-7 (hardcover)
  1. Duff, Hilary, 1987—Juvenile literature. 2. Actors—United States—Biography—Juvenile literature. I. Title.
  PN2287.D79D68 2008
  792.02'8092—dc22
  [B]
                       2007030615

ISBN-10: 1-4205-0012-0

Printed in the United States of America

Contents

Fame and celebrity are alluring. People are drawn to those who walk in fame's spotlight, whether they are known for great accomplishments or for notorious deeds. The lives of the famous pique public interest and attract attention, perhaps because their experiences seem in some ways so different from, yet in other ways so similar to, our own.

Newspapers, magazines, and television regularly capitalize on this fascination with celebrity by running profiles of famous people. For example, television programs such as *Entertainment Tonight* devote all their programming to stories about entertainment and entertainers. Magazines such as *People* fill their pages with stories of the private lives of famous people. Even newspapers, newsmagazines, and television news frequently delve into the lives of well-known personalities. Despite the number of articles and programs, few provide more than a superficial glimpse at their subjects.

Lucent's People in the News series offers young readers a deeper look into the lives of today's newsmakers, the influences that have shaped them, and the impact they have had in their fields of endeavor and on other people's lives. The subjects of the series hail from many disciplines and walks of life. They include authors, musicians, athletes, political leaders, entertainers, entrepreneurs, and others who have made a mark on modern life and who, in many cases, will continue to do so for years to come.

These biographies are more than factual chronicles. Each book emphasizes the contributions, accomplishments, or deeds that have brought fame or notoriety to the individual and shows how that person has influenced modern life. Authors portray their subjects in a realistic, unsentimental light. For example, Bill Gates—the cofounder and chief executive officer of the software giant Microsoft—has been instrumental in making personal computers the most vital tool of the modern age. Few dispute his business savvy, his perseverance, or his technical expertise, yet critics say he is ruthless in his dealings with competitors and driven more by his desire to maintain Microsoft's dominance in the computer industry than by an interest in furthering technology.

In these books, young readers will encounter inspiring stories about real people who achieved success despite enormous obstacles. Oprah Winfrey—the most powerful, most watched, and wealthiest woman on television today—spent the first six years of her life in the care of her grandparents while her unwed mother sought work and a better life elsewhere. Her adolescence was colored by promiscuity, pregnancy at age fourteen, rape, and sexual abuse.

Each author documents and supports his or her work with an array of primary and secondary source quotations taken from diaries, letters, speeches, and interviews. All quotes are footnoted to show readers exactly how and where biographers derive their information and provide guidance for further research. The quotations enliven the text by giving readers eyewitness views of the life and accomplishments of each person covered in the People in the News series.

In addition, each book in the series includes photographs, annotated bibliographies, timelines, and comprehensive indexes. For both the casual reader and the student researcher, the People in the News series offers insight into the lives of today's newsmakers—people who shape the way we live, work, and play in the modern age.

A Tween Queen Grows Up

Hilary Duff has built an empire on her wholesome, likable image. To her television career she has added projects in music, movies, and business. And she has always remained true to her own style. Duff has avoided the traps of drugs and alcohol and stays away from the Hollywood party scene. As her popularity grows, Duff remains focused on a career that is varied as well as successful.

Duff gained national stardom as an actress at age thirteen playing the clumsy and endearing Lizzie McGuire on the television show of the same name. A backstage pass to a Disney concert then sparked her interest in becoming a singer. Duff's first album, *Metamorphosis*, was a surprising success. Soon, singing was a major part of her career, as she toured and continued to record.

The young star did not let her acting career sit idle, however. She moved from television to the big screen with films such as *The Lizzie McGuire Movie* and *A Cinderella Story*. Along the way, Duff's image became a business. Before she knew it, the popular actress and singer was also earning money through the sale of Hilary Duff products. Her name and picture have helped to sell her own lines of clothing, perfume, and accessories.

Duff achieved a great deal of success as a teen and has the earnings to prove it, but fame has not been easy on her. She has many young fans applauding her work, but she also takes her share of harsh criticism. Duff endured many rejections before landing a starring role and has been criticized for the quality of her acting.

Her singing talents have also been called into question, and her wholesome image makes her a target for ridicule. Duff has learned to ignore the criticism and concentrate on her career.

Despite her success, Duff has not had a lot of time to sit back and enjoy what she has achieved. Her work, as an actress, singer, and businesswoman, has been a constant part of her life since she was a young teen. She sometimes tires of her nonstop schedule. At the same time, she admits that she enjoys her work too much to give it up. A few days away from her career has her aching to get back to acting or singing.

More challenges lie ahead for Duff as she leaves her teen years behind. She has a solid fan base of young girls, but it will be difficult for her to maintain her popularity as she grows older. As she changes from a child star to a young adult entertainer, Duff needs to develop an image that older teens and young adults can relate to. While Duff continues her career, in music, acting, and business, she is taking on a more mature look that continues to reflect her individual style.

Chapter 1

Fun, Frustration, and Lizzie McGuire

Hilary Duff began her acting career when she was still in grade school. By the time she was in middle school, she was the star of a television show. But Hilary was not born in Hollywood—she was born in Houston, Texas, on September 28, 1987.

When Hilary was young, her family lived near the small community of Boerne, Texas, about 30 miles (48km) northwest of San Antonio in the area of central Texas known as the hill country. Her family later bought a ranch in Bastrop, about 30 miles (48km) east of Austin. As a young child, Hilary spent a great deal of time outdoors, playing in the wide open spaces of the countryside.

Hilary's father, Bob, owned a chain of convenience stores and her mother, Susan, was a homemaker. Hilary has a sister, Haylie, who is two years older than she is.

When Hilary was about five years old, she began taking dance and gymnastics classes. Her first onstage experiences came through her ballet classes. At age six, she was selected to be part of the cast of the holiday season classic *The Nutcracker.*

Hilary's sister, Haylie, was also part of the cast. The sisters showed some promise as dancers, but they did not use dancing as a route to their careers in the entertainment industry. Haylie wanted to take acting lessons. After she became interested in acting, Hilary followed. "When I was a little girl

I didn't think this is what I wanted to do," Hilary said when she was a teenager. "My older sister actually wanted to be an actress and singer and of course being the younger sister I wanted to do everything she did."[1]

Commercial Success

Hilary and her sister quickly moved from their interest in acting classes to auditioning for roles. Their first parts came in television commercials, when Hilary was about six years old. Hilary, her mother, and her sister traveled from Texas to California for auditions. The girls easily won parts. It seemed to Hilary and her family that getting acting jobs was effortless.

The girls enjoyed acting so much that they begged their mother to let them move to California. Living there would make it easier for them to audition for roles in commercials and television shows. Their mother was not against the idea because she saw that her daughters seemed to be natural actresses. Their father did not want to leave Texas, however. His business was based there and he wanted to stay.

The family came to a compromise. Hilary, Haylie, and their mother made the move to California and their father stayed in Texas to look after his business. They made plans to have him visit every few weeks. Both of Hilary's parents saw that their daughters were passionate about becoming actresses. They wanted to give them every opportunity to achieve their dream.

In 1996, when Hilary was nine, she moved to Los Angeles with her mother and sister. To make her new surroundings seem like home, the family also brought their pets: a hermit crab, a gerbil, two goldfish, and a rabbit. Hilary's family moved in time to audition for pilot shows that were being made for the next television season.

Susan Duff became her daughters' manager, and the girls soon had a number of auditions lined up. Hilary and Haylie expected that winning a role in a television show would be as easy as getting roles in commercials. But they soon found out otherwise.

Reality Sets In

Hilary was enthusiastic about working as an actress. Both she and her sister tried hard to win 6roles, but they faced a lot of rejection. "... [Y]ou audition and you audition and you don't get anything,"[2] Hilary said.

She and Haylie both won small roles in the 1997 television miniseries *True Women,* a romantic Western. Their parts in the show were so tiny that their characters did not even have names. That same year, Haylie also got another small role in the television movie *Hope*, and the next year Hilary got a small role in the romantic comedy movie *Playing by Heart.*

With parts being hard to come by and both girls auditioning for roles, the possibility for jealousy existed when one sister got a part and the other did not. Their parents realized this and addressed it right away. They did not want acting to turn their daughters into enemies so their father issued an ultimatum. He told them that if they ever fought over a part they would have to return home to Texas.

Hilary said it was an asset to have a sister who was also interested in acting and show business. At home their games turned into shows, as they dressed up and took on different parts. "We would play in our bedrooms every single night together, act out scenes we saw in movies, play dress up together and act like we were someone else," Hilary said.[3]

Casper Meets Wendy

In 1998, Haylie got a part in *Addams Family Reunion.* That same year, Hilary got her first starring role. Things finally seemed to be taking off for the young actress when she got the lead role in the video movie *Casper Meets Wendy.*

The movie combined live action and animation and had a child-friendly plot that involved Casper and Wendy working together to overcome an evil warlock. The movie was released on video and wasn't a major motion picture, but it did give Hilary the opportunity to work with film veterans. Experienced actors Teri Garr, Shelly Duvall, and George Hamilton also had parts in the film.

Getting Her Goat

When Hilary was making *Casper Meets Wendy,* she tried hard to follow instructions from the director. In one scene she had to chase a goat, and the director kept yelling, "Meaner, Meaner." Hilary's expression got angrier and she ran faster as she chased the goat.

Finally the director stopped the scene and asked Hilary what she was doing. He had not meant for her to look so mad. Rather than telling her how to act, he was simply calling out the name of the goat—which happened to be Meaner.

The video also gave Hilary additional exposure as an actress. Her smiling face, alongside a cartoon image of Casper, appeared on the cover of the video. The role also brought Hilary her first praises as a professional actress. She was nominated for a Young Artist Award in the category of Best Performance in a TV Movie/Pilot/Mini-Series or Series for an actor age ten or under. When Hilary became a teen, she was embarrassed by the role but admitted she learned a great deal while making the movie.

Award Winner

Hilary's next role won her an award. In 1999, she appeared in the television movie *Soul Collector.* The film was about an angel of death who helps a woman dealing with trouble on her farm. The movie starred former child actress Melissa Gilbert, and Hilary played the part of Ellie.

Hilary's performance was notable enough to earn her a Young Artist Award for Best Performance in a TV Movie or Pilot—Supporting Young Actress. The roles Hilary was getting were small ones, but she made the most of them. She was not getting many roles, but she was being applauded for the work she did.

However, just when it seemed that Hilary's career was set to take off, frustration set in. Roles again became difficult to come by for the young actress. In 2000, she appeared in an episode of the television series *Chicago Hope*, a drama set in a Chicago hospital. She played Jessie Seldon in an episode called "Cold Hearts." But although Hilary got this small part, she was not having much success at other auditions.

TV Frustrations

Even when Hilary got a part, things did not always go her way. She was cast as one of the children in the pilot episode for the sitcom *Daddio*. The show starred Michael Chiklis as Chris Woods, a dad who decided to leave his job to stay home with his children.

Things looked good when the show was picked up by NBC. However, Hilary was dropped from the cast before the first show aired. It may have been some comfort to her that the show did not go on to become a hit. It lasted for only nine episodes before it was pulled from the network's schedule.

By now Hilary knew that rejection was part of being an actress. But that did not make it easier for the thirteen-year-old to accept. Hilary still liked acting, but she was disappointed at being turned down for so many roles. It hurt when she was dropped from the cast even after she got a part. She was frustrated with the process but decided to go on one last audition. "I was, like, wanting to quit," she said, "and I had one audition left, and it was Lizzie McGuire."[4]

If at First You Don't Succeed

At first, Hilary was not even sure she wanted to audition for *Lizzie McGuire*. She was home in Texas when she heard that Disney wanted her to audition for the show. She was tired of going to failed auditions and did not want to put herself through that again.

Hilary's sunny personality and "average teen" attitude won over the Lizzie McGuire executives.

Eventually, however, Hilary changed her mind. She realized she could see her friends in Los Angeles if she went back, and do the audition as well. With those thoughts in mind, she tried out for the part.

The initial meeting with the casting director confirmed Hilary's worst fears. The reading did not go well. The casting director said she was unprepared. He hinted that she needed an acting coach. Hilary was embarrassed by the audition, but there was a bright side. These drawbacks were not enough to prevent her from getting called back to do another reading for the role.

Eye-catching Style

When Hilary auditioned for *Lizzie McGuire*, she had to go to four auditions before she got the part. One executive said that her fashionable wardrobe had something to do with her being called back so many times. "She wasn't doing anything wrong," said Rich Ross, who was president of the channel's entertainment division. "She just wore such great outfits, and we wanted to see what she'd come in with next."

Kate Stroup, "Girl Power," *Newsweek*, March 17, 2003, p. 56.

There was something about Hilary's personality that the show's executives liked. They were looking for someone who was an average kid, not a cheerleader, jock, or geek, but just a normal teen. They called Hilary back again and again for auditions. By the fourth time, they knew that Hilary would make a great Lizzie. The show's creator, Terri Minsky, said that the way Hilary approached the character's problems got her the role. She could "make all those early teen traumas seem not so scary, very relatable."[5] Hilary gladly accepted the offer to play Lizzie McGuire.

Here's Lizzie

Lizzie McGuire began airing in January 2001 on the Disney Channel. Hilary was thirteen and so was the character she played. Hilary brought a level of believability to the role. She was the right age and had the proper attitude to deal with the difficult world of middle school.

The show had an added twist that brought both warmth and humor to its plots. Every once in awhile an animated version of Lizzie would step in to voice the character's concerns, fears, and

When Hilary started playing the role of Lizzie McGuire, she was the same age as the character—13.

regrets. This allowed the series to not only show what happened to Lizzie, but to include her thoughts about her experiences. In addition to playing the Lizzie McGuire character, Hilary also voiced the animated version.

The show took its plot lines from the troublesome world of middle school. It drew on themes of growing up, friendship, and responsibility. Along with her friends Gordo and Miranda, played by Adam Lamberg and Lalaine Dupree, Lizzie dealt with crises that many middle school–age kids could relate to. For example, in the first episode Lizzie became upset at not being chosen for the cheerleading squad and made up a story about one of the cheerleaders stuffing her bra. The story spread, and Lizzie had to own up to her mistake. *Lizzie McGuire* used events that students could identify with. In one episode, Lizzie agonized over what to wear on picture day. Things got worse when her parents make her put on a unicorn sweater given to her by her grandmother. Other episodes brought up the subject of boy-girl relationships. A class assignment about marriage made Lizzie upset. She became jealous when her friend Miranda was paired with a boy Lizzie had a crush on. In the end, Lizzie learned that friendship is more valuable than a crush.

In addition to dealing with troubles at school, Lizzie had a troublesome younger brother (played by Jake Thomas). He did such things as turning their home into the McGuire Museum of Dirt, Stains, and Slime and bringing people home to see it. Although Lizzie encountered awkward situations, she handled

Oops!

Like Lizzie, Hilary had her share of embarrassing moments. When she was signing autographs at a Disney concert, she got up to take a break and returned to her chair without realizing it had been moved. She started to sit down—with no chair under her. She fell in front of everyone.

them in a believable and entertaining way. This made the show popular from the beginning.

Hilary said she could identify with her character. If Lizzie McGuire were a real person, Hilary said they would be friends. Hilary was more self-confident than Lizzie, she said, but added that they had similar tastes in fashion and in friends.

A Hit

Lizzie McGuire premiered to positive reviews. Laura Fries of *Daily Variety* called it "beguiling and entertaining" and said it deserved to be shown in a better time slot. She liked its use of animation and its peek into Lizzie's thoughts. "The result is an amusing slice-of-life comedy that deserves a place in primetime instead of a dinnertime spot on Disney's Friday schedule,"[6] she said.

Audiences agreed. At the time it aired, *Lizzie McGuire* was the Disney Channel's highest rated show. And it wasn't only kids who enjoyed it. Lizzie's funny, wholesome, and sincere attitude appealed to parents as well. Hilary credited the show's success to its focus on teen issues. "Girls are just trying to find out who they are at this stage, and that's totally what Lizzie is about,"[7] she said.

The creator of the show, Terri Minsky, said Hilary also had something to do with the show being a hit. She carried off the role in a way that made the scenes believable, whether she was being sprayed with ketchup or dealing with boys. She "captures every emotion you remember living yourself,"[8] Minsky said.

The show's success brought Hilary some job security. Disney initially ordered twenty shows, but less than a month after the show began airing, an additional ten were ordered. The summer after *Lizzie McGuire* premiered on the Disney Channel, it also began airing on ABC on Saturday morning.

Fame for Hilary

Suddenly, Hilary was a star. She had gone from being frustrated by continued rejection to being the lead actor in a successful

After so many rejections, becoming such a success was a surprise for Hilary.

series. In late 2001, *The Hollywood Reporter* named her as one of four child actors to keep an eye on. The publication noted that Hilary and the show had received more than seven million e-mails during the first eleven months *Lizzie McGuire* aired.

It was not long before fans began to recognize Hilary in public. Her face was no longer anonymous. She could not go to the mall without people asking for her autograph.

The loss of privacy was a surprise for Hilary, who hoped for a career as an actress. She did not expect fame to come so quickly. Sudden stardom was a weird experience for the teen. "There's really no way to prepare yourself for it," she said. "It just kind of hits."[9]

Chapter 2

Tween Queen

The success of *Lizzie McGuire* helped Hilary build a career. Failed auditions became a faded memory as she became a working actress with a television show and movie offers. The popularity of her character soon took her fame beyond television. Disney introduced a marketing campaign that included books, clothing, and other products based on her character. Soon Hilary was reaching beyond *Lizzie McGuire* into movies and music.

Although Hilary was no longer dealing with a series of frustrating auditions, she and her family still found it difficult to handle the entertainment industry. Hilary's mother was one of the people helping to manage her acting career, which was briefly affected by a split with Disney. This situation was not ideal, but Hilary persevered. *Lizzie McGuire* brought her a fan base and Hilary used it to launch a varied career.

Lizzie's Everywhere

The success of *Lizzie McGuire* led to a marketing campaign based on the character Hilary played. The tween market, aimed at children age ten to thirteen, was filled with products dedicated to her. A series of chapter books, with Hilary's picture on the cover, took Lizzie and her problems to young readers. There were dolls children could use to create their own Lizzie situations, as well as a video game. And kids could buy Lizzie stickers, shirts, pillow covers, and a board game called "What Would Lizzie Do?"

Disney heavily promoted the show, calling 2002 the "Summer of Lizzie." Frisbees with the name of the show were thrown

Hilary's *Lizzie McGuire* Ideas

In an interview with Alicia Clott for *Girls' Life* magazine, Hilary gave her own thoughts on what she would like Lizzie McGuire to tackle next. She thought it would be funny to take her character in a whole new direction. When asked what storyline she would write for the character, she said. "Lizzie and her friends become superheroes, like Charlie's Angels, and kick some villain's butt!"

Clott also asked Hilary about Lizzie's future school plans. "I don't know about Lizzie, but Hilary is hitting high school," Hilary said. "I can't believe I am going to be a freshman. If Lizzie goes to high school, I think she'll be excited but nervous. There could be some really funny confrontations with the upper classmen."

Alicia Clott, *Girls' Life*, April/May 2002, p. 45.

around at beaches, and a marathon of Lizzie shows was broadcast in July. New episodes of the show were also ordered for fall 2002.

Fame's Flip Side

Hilary enjoyed working on *Lizzie McGuire*. The episodes were filmed on a set in the heart of Hollywood, and the people who worked on the show made the set a welcoming place. Some of the adults Hilary worked with even brought their dogs to work with them. This gave the set a relaxed atmosphere that helped Hilary to feel at home.

Although Hilary loved her job, she was not as comfortable with all the attention that came along with her role on a popular show. She was fairly shy in public. However, Hilary did not mind it

Dating Aaron Carter became news—and then it turned scary for Hilary.

when boys and girls approached her to talk. She also liked getting letters from fans. As the show became more popular, however, the press picked up some details about her personal life. She got an early lesson about the backlash of fame when a teenage crush turned into a news story.

Hilary began dating Aaron Carter, a singer with hits such as "Crush on You." Aaron appeared on the *Lizzie McGuire* show in 2001 and had a following among young girls. After he and Hilary began dating, some girls saw Hilary as an enemy. They did not appreciate her becoming a part of Aaron's life.

The romance did not last long. It soon turned into an on-again, off-again relationship. After Aaron began dating actress Lindsay Lohan, stories also emerged about a feud between Lindsay and Hilary. Hilary was surprised at the attention her brief relationship and breakup with Aaron generated. She vowed never to date anyone in the entertainment industry again. "When I started dating (Aaron), girls hated me so much that it was scary," she said.[10]

Budding Musical Interest

The end of her relationship with Aaron and her reported feud with Lindsay did not distract Hilary from her work. She was much too busy to think about romance or rumors of a fight. When a reporter asked about her relationship with Aaron, she explained, "The deal is we have an on-again/off-again friendship," she said. "Aaron is a player, and I'm not."[11]

A new interest helped Hilary fill her time in 2001: singing. Her sister was part of a band, and watching her rehearse attracted Hilary's attention. After being part of a Radio Disney concert in 2001, Hilary was so impressed by the talent of the performers in the show that she decided to move in that direction with her career. "There were all these pop acts backstage at the concert," Hilary said. "They were all getting ready backstage and warming up, and I was like, 'I want to do this so bad.'"[12]

At the concert she met Andre Recke, who would help manage her music career. Recke instantly felt that Hilary had the personality to help her succeed in this new venture. "When I met Hilary, I knew she had something special," Recke said. "Sometimes you just have that feeling, that, 'Wow, she's a star.'"[13]

Hilary had taken voice lessons when she was a student at a performing arts school but had stopped once her acting career took off. Although Hilary had not had a strong interest in music when she was younger, she was ready to return to singing. She took singing lessons in an effort to improve her voice. Hilary wanted to be ready for opportunities to test her vocal abilities.

Can't Wait

Hilary's connection with Disney gave the teen her first chance to be a singer. She worked with several producers to record *I Can't Wait*, an upbeat pop tune. The song was included on the *Lizzie McGuire* CD (a collection of songs from the television show released in August 2002) and was played on Radio Disney. The CD featured a smiling Hilary on the cover and included songs by Jessica Simpson, Smash Mouth, and Mandy Moore.

In September, the *Disneymania* CD was released and featured a number of artists singing well-known Disney songs. *NSYNC did "When You Wish Upon a Star," Ashanti performed "Colors of the Wind," and Aaron Carter contributed "I Just Can't Wait to be King." Christina Aguilera and Smash Mouth were also featured on the CD, and alongside them was Hilary with her rendition of "The Tiki, Tiki, Tiki Room." "That was the first test to see how her fans would react to her as a singer and not just as an actress," Recke said.[14]

Hilary's singing was a hit with her fans and Disney decided she should have her own CD. In October 2002, the Christmas CD *Santa Claus Lane* was released. Haylie Duff, Hilary's sister and a member of the band Inventing Venus, contributed to the CD as a songwriter. In addition to the title track, the CD included classics such as "Jingle Bell Rock" and "Santa Claus is Coming to Town." Other singers who children related to were also featured on the CD, such as Lil' Romeo and Christina Milian. The CD reached No. 2 on Billboard's top Kids Albums and Top Heatseekers charts and was re-released in 2003 with an added track.

The Lizzie McGuire CD was Hilary's first chance to be a singer.

Becoming Hilary

Hilary did not want to be known only as Lizzie McGuire, and music was one way she could distance herself from the character. Hilary's face was on many Lizzie McGuire products but her name was not. People sometimes thought her real name was Lizzie McGuire. The confusion came from the popularity of the television show and the products associated with it. Hilary wanted people to start to realize that she was not the same person as the character she played. On the CDs she sang under her own name, and the *Disneymania* and *Santa* albums had no connection to Hilary's television show.

Disney began to promote Hilary as an individual on other programs as well. In 2002 and 2003, Hilary made appearances on the Nickelodeon Kids' Choice Awards. She was also part of

Fantastic Fans

Soon after *Lizzie McGuire* appeared on television, Hilary began receiving letters from fans and began being recognized in public. Teens and preteens made up the majority of her admirers. Hilary's mom, Susan Duff, said they seemed more like friends than fans, because they knew so much about Hilary. One fan came up to Hilary and her mother at a restaurant and the little girl proceeded to tell Hilary that she loved her show and knew the name of her best friend (Taylor), her mom (Susan) and her dog (Little Dog). "She knew everything," Susan Duff said. "It was so adorable!"

Other fans tried to get Hilary's attention in odd ways. When she was hosting TRL at MTV studios, one young man arrived wearing an outfit that looked like a giant hot dog bun. He carried a sign that said. "I dressed up as a hot dog for you. I'm a dork!"

Tim Carvell, "The Girl in the Bubble," *Entertainment Weekly*, May 9, 2003, p. 34.
Mark Dagostino, et al, "Tween Queen," *People*, May 19, 2003, p. 83.

the Walt Disney World Christmas Day parade. Her television show appearances included the MTV Video Music Awards, the American Music Awards, and the Teen Choice Awards. The busy teen was a co-host of the Total Request Live All-Star Backyard BBQ. Hilary was also featured on segments of *Good Morning America* and *Punk'd*.

Hilary was far from the only star popular with young girls. In addition to making sure people knew she was not the character she played on television, she had to set herself apart from other young stars as well. Entertainers such as Britney Spears, Mary-Kate and Ashley Olsen, and Avril Lavigne all had music, movies, or products that did well in the tween market. Hilary established her niche by simply being herself. She was more wholesome than Britney, and was a singer, unlike the Olsens. Her optimistic music

Both Hilary and sister Haylie appeared on the Teen Choice Awards.

was the opposite of the edgy songs by Avril. Hilary was happy with who she was and let her upbeat style come through.

Moving to Movies

In addition to starting a music career, Hilary also expanded her acting career. She moved into movie roles that took her beyond her Lizzie McGuire character. After a small role in the 2001 movie *Human Nature*, the next year Hilary got a lead part in the Disney Channel movie *Cadet Kelly*. In that film she played a girl trying to fit in at a strict military school.

Preparing for the role meant going through a week of intensive military training. Hilary then went to Toronto for four weeks of rehearsal before filming began. Hilary did her own stunts for the movie, and she learned how to do drill team moves that involved tossing rifles. Although she almost knocked herself out a few times, she enjoyed the rehearsals.

Hilary's image made her seem like a girl who was more interested in makeup than athletics. However, she liked the physical challenges in *Cadet Kelly*. She claimed she could make it through boot camp, if they let her keep her lip gloss. "It was great fun, and I can arm wrestle with the best now," she said. "I am pretty athletic, and I like a challenge."[15]

The movie was popular with Disney Channel viewers even though it failed to get good reviews. Reviewer David Nusair called it "extraordinarily predictable, utterly routine," but admitted that "young girls will probably appreciate Duff's spunky, spirited performance."[16] Although Hilary tried to distance herself from Lizzie McGuire with *Cadet Kelly*, Nusair said it seemed like she was playing the same character.

Cody Banks

Hilary made another attempt to step into a different character with a supporting role in the 2003 film *Agent Cody Banks*, starring Frankie Muniz. Hilary played the daughter of a scientist, and

Muniz was a secret agent trying to stop her father from destroying the Earth. Hilary's character was more self-assured than Lizzie McGuire, but the movie's audience was the same as Lizzie's.

Once again, Hilary's movie was a success with kids, tweens and young teens. "'Agent' is an amusing, semi-exciting, gadget-filled spy comedy aimed squarely at tweeners (those too old for Elmo but too young for 007)," reviewer Leah Rozen wrote.[17] The movie revived public interest in Hilary's social life as well, as she briefly dated the movie's star, Muniz. But this time the brief romance did not generate any ill will among their fans.

Doing it All

Hilary had a busy schedule that included movies, music, and school. She had little time to devote to her personal life. She was so busy that she barely had time to even go shopping at the mall. On work days she had to get up at 5:30 A.M. and was on the set by 7 A.M. to deal with wardrobe, makeup, and hairstyling. After scenes were shot, she had to spend three hours with an on-set tutor, and change from acting to studying. When doing the *Lizzie McGuire* episodes she also had to find time to record lines for the animated Lizzie.

Hilary's day on the set of *Lizzie McGuire* ended at around 4:30 P.M. Then, in the evening, she had to learn her lines for the next day, do homework, and attend an exercise class. Hilary also had voice lessons. She tried to get to bed by 9:30 P.M., to get enough sleep to have energy for the next day.

Making movies often took Hilary away from her family's homes in Los Angeles and Texas. To make life on the road a little more like home, she brought photos of her family and friends with her. She took an old stuffed animal with her as well. Hilary remained upbeat about her situation, realizing that it took sacrifice if she was to do the job she enjoyed. "When I do movies, I don't see my friends for a few months, but I love my job," she said. "So it pays off."[18]

Hilary was a teen with a glamorous full-time job, but her mother tried to keep her daughter's fame from going to her

In 2003 Hilary appeared in Agent Cody Banks with Frankie Muniz.

A Dog's Life

Hilary and her family came to Los Angeles with a number of pets. Once they arrived, they brought a dog into their home as well. Hilary's dog, Little Dog, lived a pretty easy life. If Hilary could trade places with anyone for a day, she said it would be her dog. "She totally has the life," Hilary said. "Her day consists of lying around sleeping, eating, sunning and being pampered. I think I could deal with that!"

Hilary later got a Chihuahua named Lola and loved to dress her puppy in style. She visited L.A. clothing boutiques to buy outfits for her pet. "I probably spend $150 on a dress," she said. "She's spoiled." She also bought hot pink and cheetah print carrying pouches for her pet. She noted that the dog could tell when they were no longer brand new. "Once you wash them a couple of times, they're not as soft," Hilary said. "She won't even get in. She's like, 'Uh-uh.'"

Alicia Clott, *Girls' Life*, April/May 2002, p. 45.
Molly Lopez, *People*, August 1, 2005, p. 104.

head. She did this by making sure Hilary had chores to do at home. Hilary had to clean her room and take out the garbage. Sometimes Hilary's life mirrored that of a typical teen: homework, arguments with her sister, or a disagreement with her mom over cleaning her room. However, during the week, her life was anything but normal.

Lizzie on the Big Screen

Although Hilary's life was different from the lives of most kids her age, Hilary still acted like a typical teen. This was part of her appeal. It was also what made her television series so successful. As Hilary grew older, her character grew as well. Lizzie's graduation from middle school provided the series with an excuse to move beyond television.

Dogs and other animals have always been a part of Hilary's life.

The popular series was turned into a big-screen picture, *The Lizzie McGuire Movie,* in 2003. The film gave Hilary a role that included singing as well as acting. It also gave her the opportunity to play a character other than Lizzie, as the movie's plot included an Italian Lizzie look-alike named Isabella.

The movie brought Lizzie and her classmates out of middle school and over to Europe. In Italy, Lizzie happened to meet a pop star. He noticed that she looked a great deal like his singing partner, Isabella, and he convinced her to pretend to be the singer. When Lizzie snuck out to be with the pop star, her friends wondered if she knew what she was getting herself into.

The movie's plot gave Hilary the opportunity to sing. She took the stage for "Why Not" and "What Dreams Are Made Of." The role also gave her the opportunity to make many costume changes. The fashion sequences became some of the movie's most engaging scenes. The movie was a hit with its target audience and took in $17.3 million on its opening weekend. By June, it was set to surpass $40 million. "Young fans of the TV show will relish Lizzie because the innocuously likable Duff is in every scene, modeling wacky outfits and singing," wrote Adam Lambert in *People* magazine. "Accompanying adults will be grateful there's no violence or potty humor, a rarity in kids' films today."[19]

The movie was popular with young girls and teens, but Hilary's popularity did not extend far beyond them. "Squarely aimed at the core viewers of the Disney Channel's tween favorite, the film is frilly and sweet to a mind-numbing fault," wrote reviewer David Noh in *Film Journal International.* He said Hilary looked like "more of a human Barbie doll than a normal high school kid."[20] When the movie was released, many adults were trying to figure out who this young girl was. Those who had not seen *Lizzie McGuire* on The Disney Channel appreciated her appeal, but they did not like the movie. Philip Kerr, a writer for the *New Statesman*, criticized the film for "the dreadful acting, the dreadful script, the putrid jokes, a leading lady, who it would appear, aspires to be a sponge."[21] Still, he predicted that Hilary would become a star.

The television hit turned into **The Lizzie McGuire Movie.**

Break with Disney

The Lizzie McGuire Movie was a commercial success and Hilary's popularity was growing. However, her relationship with Disney was not going well. Things quickly soured after the movie's release.

In mid-2003, Hilary and her mom had a very public split with Disney. *The Lizzie McGuire Movie* was meant to put an end to Lizzie McGuire's middle school years. It paved the way for a new series featuring Lizzie as a high school student. The planned show would be on ABC, a network owned by Disney. However, other networks also wanted to give Hilary her own prime-time series and offered her more money. Susan Duff, Hilary's mom and business manager, disagreed with Disney over how much Hilary should be paid.

The Duffs decided to part with Disney. They did not want to accept the contracts the company was offering. After sixty-five episodes as Lizzie McGuire, Hilary was done with the character.

Disney executives said they had done everything they could to work with the Duffs. Susan Duff, however, did not see it that way. "Disney thought they'd be able to bully us into accepting whatever offer they wanted to make, and they couldn't," she said. "We walked away from a sequel [to *The Lizzie McGuire Movie*]. They walked away from a franchise."[22]

A New Path

Hilary was moving on to a new chapter in her life, and the future was both exciting and scary. She no longer had a movie sequel or television series to fall back on. However, she was still a popular figure with teens and now had time to give more attention to her budding career as a singer.

Although Hilary was free to take her career in a new direction, away from Disney, things did not always go smoothly. Hilary had been working with CBS to develop a new sitcom and signed the deal in November 2003. However, writers and producers couldn't come up with the right project for her, and a new series never materialized.

But this drawback did not slow Hilary down. She had wisely extended her career beyond television. She had both movies and music to keep her busy. Hilary had learned to deal with popularity and fame while maintaining the wholesome, likable image that made her a star.

Chapter 3

Metamorphosis

The end of the *Lizzie McGuire* series was softened by Hilary's development in other areas of the entertainment industry. Hilary had wanted to move away from the Lizzie McGuire character, and the split with Disney allowed her to focus on singing, touring, and movies. She had worked hard to make Lizzie McGuire a well-known brand. Now she was ready to put that same energy into promoting herself as a singer and actress.

Hilary's family ties remained strong. Her mother continued to help manage her career, and Hilary remained supportive of her mother's decisions. Although some people questioned the Duffs' move to break away from Disney, Hilary believed in her mother's guidance. She felt her mom was doing what was best for her and her career. She said that people might call Susan Duff a stage mom, but Hilary felt that she was only stopping people from taking advantage of her.

Rebirth

Hilary's first move after leaving Disney was to concentrate on her singing career. She was no longer associated with the company's television shows but was still connected to Disney's music business. Disney's music venture Buena Vista/Hollywood Records helped her to put out her first CD, *Metamorphosis*.

Metamorphosis, released in 2003, was a way for Hilary to establish herself as a singer and a performer away from the popular character she had portrayed on television and onscreen. She was still connected with *Lizzie McGuire* in her fans' minds and would

With the release of her CD Metamorphosis, Hilary began singing in front of live audiences.

be called Lizzie if a fan recognized her on the street. Hilary did not mind being called Lizzie, but she wanted her music to be more about herself than a character. "I think that it is going to be nice to get people to get to know me better through my music," she said.[23]

The CD's title, *Metamorphosis*, meant "rebirth." It showed that Hilary was entering a new phase of her career and life. She was looking to emerge from the Lizzie McGuire cocoon and grow as a performer. Hilary wanted the songs on the CD to reflect this. She tried to create an album she could relate to with songs that weren't obvious pop tunes.

Making an album was not something Hilary could do without a great deal of assistance from people in the music industry. Songwriters and producers gathered the album's material for her. She was simply too busy to write the songs herself. "I actually didn't want to have control of the writing on my first album," she said. "To write, you have to have time to connect with yourself. I don't have that time right now."[24]

Although Hilary did not write the songs on the album, they still needed to reflect who she was. Hilary wanted to carve her own identity in music, not copy someone else. "There are definitely people I respect and I love their music, but there was never really an artist that I said, 'I want to be just like them. I love the way their career is going. I love their music,'" she said. "It wasn't really like that. I just wanted to be like myself."[25]

Selling Hilary

Hilary needed to convince radio stations that her music was hip enough for a broad teen audience, not just tweens and Radio Disney. To do this, Hilary hit the road. She met with radio station programmers to show them that her music was mature enough to get airplay. "Our biggest asset all along is Hilary herself," said record executive Abbey Konowich. "When we took her out to meet programmers, they were amazed with her poise, her smile, her passion about music and the fact that she didn't look like the twelve-year-old they were afraid she'd be."[26]

The first single released from *Metamorphosis* was "So Yesterday," a song that reflected Hilary's optimism and her ability to let go of the past. Hilary and her management team worked carefully to give the light pop song a wholesome sound with enough of an edge to receive radio airplay. The song's video was also carefully designed. It was meant to appeal to younger fans as well as MTV viewers. That single and another called "Come Clean" helped make *Metamorphosis* an immediate success. The album debuted at No. 2 and went platinum weeks after it was released in August 2003. There was fear that Hilary's CD would be too focused on young teens, but the resulting sound was appealing. *Rolling Stone* reviewer Jon Caramanica called the best songs on the CD "gleaming,"[27] and said its failures were outnumbered by its hits. *People* magazine's Chuck Arnold noted that the material on the album was not deep or filled with thought-provoking messages, but "Duff makes fairly tasty bubblegum for tweens. With a voice at least as good as that of another actress turned singer, J.Lo, and a charming girl-next-door personality that translates well from screen to record, Duff gets passable marks on pop-rock numbers like the first single, 'So Yesterday.'"[28]

Stage Fright

Hilary's transition from Lizzie McGuire to a pop sensation could not have gone more smoothly. The success of the CD proved that Hilary could be popular away from the Lizzie McGuire brand. However, once Hilary had made a CD, she had to promote it. To do this, she went on tour. At first this was an unnerving experience.

Hilary's background as an actress did not keep her from having butterflies in her stomach when she began singing in front of live audiences in fall 2003. She found that performing live onstage as a singer was quite different from acting on a movie or television set.

Hilary's fans were excited to see her in person, and her first concerts as a headliner quickly sold out. She also appeared onstage at the 2003 American Music Awards in November. It was an exciting

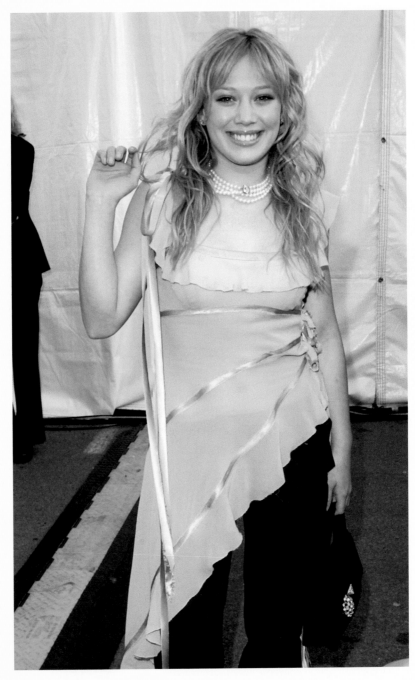

Hilary appeared onstage at the 2003 American Music Awards.

experience for her. "I felt like I had hit the big time, because I had to sing in front of all my peers," she wrote in an article in *Texas Monthly*. "I was, like, 'I can't believe I'm doing this.'"[29]

Hilary's experience of the awards show was not completely enjoyable, however. She was too nervous to get much sleep the night before she performed. On the day of the show, her stomach felt queasy. She stayed in her hotel for much of the day.

However, Hilary did get to experience the glamour of the event as she walked the red carpet, wearing a short beaded skirt with feathers. Once she got onstage, the nerves returned as she saw an older crowd rather than her young fans in the first few rows. Their presence made her feel uncomfortable, but she soon got over her awkwardness. "I got absolutely no energy from them," she said. "But I was okay once we totally rocked out and had a great time."[30]

On Tour

Many concerts followed, and Hilary was soon an experienced performer. She traveled across North America on a concert tour to promote her CD. During the Christmas season, Hilary promoted her CD in radio concerts and would sometimes do two shows in a city on the same day. Onstage, she developed a style she felt comfortable with. Although she had trained in dance when she was younger, Hilary's onstage moves were not planned. Her performing style was to feel the music and let her emotions come across naturally. "I can't say I'm (more of a) rocker than a pop girl, but if you see my (live) show, I don't dance at all," she said. "It's more like just rocking out with the band. It's not choreographed pop moves."[31]

When her concert appearances brought support from audiences, Hilary finally felt that her fans had accepted her as a singer. On tour, she enjoyed hearing people sing her songs back to her when she was onstage. The reaction was instant, and she loved it. "I had all these people supporting me," she said. "That's when I really said, 'Oh, my gosh, I'm doing it. I never thought I'd be able to perform in front of so many people.'"[32]

Still an Actress

Although Hilary had proven herself as a singer, she did not give up her acting career. However, finding roles that were both dramatic and wholesome was not an easy task. She did not want to stray too far from her clean-cut image. She wanted to play a character who was older than Lizzie, but not necessarily one who would drive young audiences away. "I know I can handle dramatic roles, but I don't think I should have to play a young mother on crack to prove it," she said.[33]

In spring 2003, Hilary filmed a supporting role in the ensemble comedy *Cheaper by the Dozen*. This remake of a 1950 movie starred Steve Martin and followed the adventures of a family with twelve children. Hilary played the third-oldest child, a part written just for her. Her character, Lorraine, was into fashion, makeup, and popularity. The size of the cast meant that Hilary had to share the screen with many other young actors and actresses. She was able to add enough depth to her character's personality, however, to make her role stand out.

Driving Tips

During the filming of *Cheaper by the Dozen*, Hilary was looking forward to getting her driver's license. Actor Tom Welling, of *Smallville* fame, played her big brother in the film and gave her some unusual driving tips. "We had a scene where we pull up to the school in a beat-up Impala while all the other kids are driving BMWs and Mercedes. He would push down on the brake and the gas at the same time. It made the car wobble." She added, "when you take your foot off the brake, the car shoots off."

Susan Wloszczyna, "For Duff's next role, the more the merrier," *USA Today*, May 23, 2003, p. 06e.

The movie was released in late 2003 and was seen by critics as a mildly funny family comedy. Critic Roger Ebert noted that Hilary's character had to endure the "usual PG-rated heartbreak" and criticized the movie for making Martin's character too predictably ambitious and bumbling. But he added, "Hey, I liked 'Cheaper by the Dozen.' These actors are skilled at being nice. It's just that the movie settles when it ought to push... it's based on sitcom families, where the most essential family value is not stepping on anybody's lines."[34]

Multitasking

Hilary had blended into the cast in *Cheaper by the Dozen*. As a performer, however, she was constantly looking for ways to stand out from the crowd. In addition to selling herself as a singer and actress, Hilary also promoted products. She had been a successful product spokesman as Lizzie McGuire, and she was equally successful at promoting products with her own name on them.

In 2004, Hilary introduced her own product line, called Stuff by Hilary Duff. She offered cosmetics, handbags, towels, and sheets as well as clothing. Hilary put her personal touch on the merchandise by helping to choose the designs for the products, which included jeans, skirts, belts, and swimsuits. She chose colors and fabric for the items, a process that was harder than she expected it to be.

Hilary did not get too involved in the day-to-day operations of the business, however. She was afraid that would be boring. The design decisions for her clothing line were more in tune with her area of expertise, because she knew what would turn kids off. One item she turned down, for example, was a swimsuit that had the word 'stuff' on it in big white letters.

Teenager of the Year

As Hilary's career grew, the amount of time she had to herself kept shrinking. She thought working on a television show had kept her busy, but movie offers, interview requests, music, and

True to Herself

Hilary had to put up with false stories being printed about her. One story said she had been drinking in a club and had begun bragging about her body. She did not need to flaunt her looks to be popular, however. "Hilary is personally a modest young woman," her mother, Susan, said. "She does not need to go around exposing herself. What you see is what you get with Hilary, basically. It almost sounds too good to be true."

Hilary did not feel pressure to be anyone except herself, and she was doing what she enjoyed. She was proud that some kids looked up to her and liked it when they asked her for advice on her Web site. "I feel like their friend," she said. "It's pretty cool."

Mark Binelli, "Teenager of the Year," *Rolling Stone*, September 18, 2003, p. 40.
Bonnie Laufer-Krebs, "The Stuff on Hilary Duff," *Teen Tribute*, Fall 2003, p. 26.

business ventures kept her busier than ever. When she was making *Cheaper by the Dozen*, she was on the set during the day and had to do three hours of school work. Then at night, she went to the studio to work on her album. However, she was convinced she could handle it all. "I don't like to rest," she said. "I'm fifteen years old. I have lots of energy."[35]

To her fans, Hilary seemed like a regular kid. Girls who stood in line for hours to get a copy of her autographed CD dressed simply like her, in jean capris. They said they liked her because she seemed real. Hilary said she really was a typical teen. Fame was unreal to her, she said, because she considered herself to be normal. Hilary's sincerity and success earned her "Teenager of the Year" honors from *Rolling Stone* magazine. "Much of Duff's success has to do with the fact that she comes off as the genuine article, a real-deal teenager," Mark Binelli said in *Rolling Stone*.[36]

With Hilary, "what you see is what you get."

Hilary had people around her who helped her manage her career and keep her humble. Her sister, mother, dad, and even her dogs helped her to stay grounded. They prevented Hilary's ego from ballooning. She got along well with her manager and had a dialogue coach who helped her deliver her lines properly. The many failed auditions she endured before landing *Lizzie McGuire* also helped to keep her ego in check. She said. "I was in L.A. working really hard since I was eight and finally it's paying off," she said. "It's just a job, just like everyone else has a job, and I think that some people don't realize that."[37]

A Busy Life

In some ways Hilary was a typical teen. She could not wait to get her driver's license and hang out with her friends. She liked going to school dances, having lunch with her sister, and jumping on a trampoline. However, her packed schedule meant she had little time to devote to her own interests. Sometimes she wished she had time to just take a day off so she could clean her room. There was no time for a boyfriend, and she also had to deal with fans coming up to her and asking for autographs. Hilary's schedule sometimes became so packed that she did not bother to look ahead. She concentrated on what she had to do at that minute. "Sometimes I won't even know what I'm doing the next day, and I'll just have to go do it and be told right before I run on," she said. "But I love that. I tell my mom when I'm tired and burned out. ... But after a week of me not working, I'm like, 'I have to get back to work, what can I do?' You know? I really don't like to not work."[38]

Hilary could not deny that she loved acting and performing. It was this strong interest that brought her back to the set, studio, and stage even when she was tired. The stress of working sometimes bothered her, but whenever she tried to quit she would get bored.

"You have those days when you're stressed out and you haven't had a day off for, like, two years and it's insane and you're like, 'Why do I do this? I could be normal!' But

Fans were always eager to get Hilary's autograph.

Letting it Out

In an interview with Lori Berger from *CosmoGirl* magazine, Hilary admitted that she did not feel her best every day. "I have days when I have big bags under my eyes, and I just don't want to wake up and face the day. I get zits and bad hair just like everyone else," she said. "But I think you have to work through it. I'm very into embracing your flaws and knowing that you're beautiful for a lot of different reasons besides just what you look like on the outside."

When things got to be too much, there was nothing like a good cry to set things right. "Sometimes there's so much going on that you just have to let it out," Hilary said. "I think I have about two really good cries a year about being so overwhelmed and having so much stress. Sometimes you don't even know what you're crying about because you've held it inside for so long. But it feels so good after!"

Lori Berger, "Hilary Duff," *CosmoGirl*, March 2004, p. 126.

then you have three days off, and you're like, 'Oh, my God, I have to get back to work!' It's almost like an addiction. I love performing."[39]

Hilary could not imagine a life without her career. Because she loved it, she continued to make the most of her work by taking on roles that enhanced her likable image.

Chapter 4

Ready for a Challenge

Hilary had ventured successfully into music and now wanted to challenge herself as an actress. She looked to broaden her acting skills by taking on roles that were more dramatic than she had done in the past. However, she was also aware that her fans expected her to entertain them with an upbeat message. Hilary knew she had to balance her desire to try new things with the realization that she would not be considered for roles that strayed too far from her image.

While Hilary pursued more movie roles, she continued her other ventures as well. She promoted her clothing and cosmetics lines, did a singing tour with her sister, and prepared to make another CD. Sometimes, she was able to combine her interests and perform music for the movies she appeared in. As a sixteen-year-old, Hilary had plenty of options in front of her. She did not want to choose between them. "I have no idea where I'm going to be in three years," she said. "But hopefully I'll be able to keep doing movies, and I think I'm going to start filming a pilot for a TV show, and I want to keep touring, and I want to do it all!"[40]

Cinderella Story

Although Hilary had left her Lizzie McGuire character behind, the strong showing of *The Lizzie McGuire Movie* continued to be

Hilary starred with Chad Michael Murray in A Cinderella Story.

an advantage for her. Hilary's name brought young girls into the movie theater. This helped her to get a lead role over a number of other young actresses in the movie *A Cinderella Story*. Hilary received $2 million for her work in the film.

The movie was an updated telling of the traditional fairy tale. Hilary played a girl with an evil stepmother who forced Hilary to work as a waitress. Hilary had an online relationship with her Prince Charming, a fellow student who hoped to attend Princeton University. They corresponded via e-mail and text messages. After they met in person, she tried to keep her identity hidden because she was afraid he would find out that she was a wait-ress. His only clue to her name was a cell phone she dropped at a school dance.

Chad Michael Murray played Austin Ames, her love interest, and Hilary got the role of Sam Montgomery. She was excited to play a character that was slightly different from Lizzie McGuire. While Lizzie McGuire had been very much like Hilary in real life, this time she was stepping into a character that required her to tone down her perky personality. "I'm hyper, she's more calm, reserved," Hilary said. "It's definitely a challenge."[41]

Hilary liked the role because it let her play a powerful char-acter who believed in herself. Changing her acting style was not easy, however. Her acting coach, Troy Rowland, worried at times that Hilary wasn't letting enough of her character's personality come through onscreen. He made Hilary watch a crying scene from the movie *Erin Brokovich,* with Julia Roberts, to show Hilary how powerful a dramatic acting performance could be.

Competition

While Hilary put a great deal of effort into her role, *A Cinderella Story* faced stiff competition at the theater when it was released in summer 2004. A number of movies aimed at the tween and young teen market opened around the same time. They included *Mean Girls* with Lindsay Lohan, *New York Minute* with the Olsen twins, and *Ella Enchanted* with Anne Hathaway. The

Haylie, left, is one of her sister's biggest supporters.

same girls who were Hilary's fans were also likely to enjoy the other films. They had to decide which movies were worth their time and money.

Faced with so much competition, *A Cinderella Story* finished in the middle of the pack. The movie was not as clever or edgy as *Mean Girls* or as silly as *New York Minute*. Although the film did not get rave reviews, the combination of Hilary and Chad Michael Murray was a good one. The movie succeeded in entertaining its target audience. The film got two stars in a *People Weekly* review and a grade C- in *Entertainment Weekly*, although reviewer Lisa Schwarzbaum was not at all enthusiastic about the picture. "When not unnecessarily bland, synthetic and undistinguishable from undistinguished teen TV, *A Cinderella Story* is unnecessarily coarse and dumbed down, with every character except Sam and Austin subject to perfunctory ridicule," she wrote. "Duff, an appealing, well-scrubbed, sixteen-year-old phenom, appears imprisoned in her own magic kingdom of carefully chaperoned celebrity."[42]

Dual Careers

Although young girls enjoyed her movies, Hilary was not a critical favorite. She had to deal with her share of disappointments when it came to her acting career. There was talk that she would have a role in the movie *Confessions of a Teenage Drama Queen*, but the part went to Lindsay Lohan. A deal for another television series also fell through.

Her mediocre movie reviews and other acting disappointments did not dampen Hilary's singing career, however. In addition to acting in *A Cinderella Story*, Hilary also performed six of the fourteen songs in the soundtrack. One of them was "Our Lips are Sealed." She performed with her sister, Haylie, who had a singing career of her own with the band Inventing Venus.

An interest in music was one of the things Hilary and Haylie had in common. They toured North America together in summer 2004. They hoped to make a movie together and perform the music for it as well. Far from being jealous, Haylie

Both Hilary, top, and Haylie pursued singing careers.

Support From Sis

Haylie Duff was one of her sister's biggest supporters. "She is just so talented," Haylie commented to a reporter. Although Haylie had developed an interest in acting before her sister did, she was not jealous when her sister's career took off. "I know that my time will come," she said, "and so meantime, I'm just happy to watch Hilary enjoy everything that's coming her way."

While the two got along well, they did not pretend to be exactly alike. They had their differences, especially when it came to being neat. "She was always the slob, and I was always the neat freak," Hilary said. "I make sure my pillows are on the bed the right way."

Nick Duerden, "The Golden Girl," *Blender*, October 2004, http://www.blender.com/guide/articles.aspx?id=1052.
Hilary Duff, Haylie Duff, "The Power Duff Girls," *People Weekly*, August 2, 2004, p. 77.

said she enjoyed watching her sister's career success. "It's been so great, and it's been crazy," she said. "I think she's handled it better than anybody in her age range. She was so young and she handled it so well. She could have been snobby, but she's not." [43]

Controversial Comments

Not everyone had such an upbeat view of Hilary's personality. The song "Our Lips Are Sealed" was a good one for the sisters to record, Hilary said, because of the stories of tiffs between her and other teen entertainers. In addition to her spat with Lindsay Lohan, sparks also flew when Hilary made a comment about singer Avril Lavigne.

Hilary said that Lavigne should have more respect for her fans, and Lavigne responded by calling her "such a goody-goody,

There were stories of bad feelings between Hilary and Avril Lavigne, top, and Lindsay Lohan, bottom.

such a mommy's girl."[44] She later added that Hilary should not criticize her because she was more of an actress than a musician and had other people write songs for her. Hilary later tried to smooth things over, saying she should not have commented on Lavigne—that she had never met her and was a fan of her music.

Although Hilary tired of the stories, talk of bad feelings between her and Lindsay Lohan also persisted. Their feud dated back to their relationships with Aaron Carter. Hilary reportedly asked that Lohan leave when she attended the premier of the movie *Cheaper by the Dozen*. Hilary's representative said the media had exaggerated the stories of disagreements between Hilary and Lohan. Lohan agreed that it was time to end their difficulties. "Things get dragged on by the public because people are interested in making things bigger than they are, but it should be let go," she said. "It's immature. It's silly. I'm sure she doesn't like me for whatever her reasons are, but I have no problem with her."[45]

An Example

Despite the stories of bad feelings between Hilary and these entertainers, Hilary never lost sight of who she was. She did not mind

Support for Mom

Because of the way she ran her daughter's career, Susan Duff was sometimes seen as a tough businesswoman. However, Hilary denied that she was a stage mom. "I love my mom," Hilary said. "I totally look up to her, and she just doesn't let anybody take advantage of me. People might call that a stage mom."

Rebecca Winters, "Q & A with Hilary Duff," *Time*, July 19, 2004, p. 89.

that Lavigne criticized her for being a good girl, because that was how she thought of herself. She did not apologize for her behavior. She tried to set an example for other teens to follow. "I look up to my mom and my sister. I'm so close to them, and they've set such a great example for me," she said. "And I want to encourage kids…to look up to people who have changed the world. We've never changed the world. Look at astronauts or doctors or Nelson Mandela."

Hilary's words of encouragement sometimes surprised other teen performers. While she was being interviewed alongside rapper Bow Wow, he admitted to having no such thoughts. "Dang, I look up to DMX and Snoop," he said. Hilary wasted no time in saying, "Oh, Bow Wow! I'm setting an example here!"[46]

Hilary knew she was not perfect. She admitted to splashing out on shopping sprees and Louis Vuitton bags, and she planned to get a nice car. She had a weakness for makeup, and could spend two hours in front of the mirror putting it on. She bought so many shoes she needed to add more storage space to her house. But when Bow Wow said he chartered a jet for $45,000 and bought two cars, her expenditures looked small. Her mom noted that Hilary's image reflected the person she was inside. "Hilary is a modest young woman," says her mom. "What you see is what you get."[47]

Dramatic Role

There were times when Hilary's positive, wholesome image made some aspects of her career difficult, however. When it came to looking for movie roles, Hilary wanted to try something that was more dramatic and edgy. In the movie *Raise Your Voice,* released in 2004, Hilary took a step in that direction. Although the movie about kids at a music camp was definitely aimed at a young audience, it gave Hilary the opportunity to take on a more mature, dramatic role. "People really haven't seen me do this kind of role before," she said.[48]

In the movie, Hilary played a small-town girl who loved to sing and was given the opportunity to attend a competitive

Raise Your Voice *was a more dramatic role for Hilary.*

summer music program in Los Angeles. At home her character dealt with a disapproving father and the tragic death of her brother, and at the camp she had to figure out how to fit in among her formally trained counterparts. "This role is definitely more dramatic, which is a good step for me," she said. "I've been playing the girl next door, but I want to do other things. It's just a matter of time."[49]

Raise Your Voice also gave her an opportunity to sing, and the part called for her to do it poorly as well as polished. Singing off-key was more difficult than doing it the right way, she said, because she liked to try to please the people she was around. Singing the wrong way embarrassed her.

Her singing, however, proved to be the sole bright spot of her performance, said critic Owen Gleiberman of *Entertainment Weekly*. He enjoyed the musical numbers, but had no respect for Hilary's talent as an actress. "The scrubbed earnestness she displays in a movie like *Raise Your Voice* seems less a personality than a plea for attention," reviewer Owen Gleiberman said. "She's as emotionally dynamic as an Oreo cookie—a programmed flirt on the outside who's all sweetness and light on the inside." [50]

People magazine found some good qualities in the movie, however, noting that although the picture was not especially captivating, it did provide girls with someone to look up to. "Duff may be sitcom-bland, but there could be worse role models for your kids," noted its review, which gave the movie two stars. "In *Raise Your Voice,* the likable teen queen gives her dramatic muscles a workout. Duff cries, pouts, sings—all passably well." [51]

Hilary Duff

It was not easy for Hilary to blend into the characters she played in her movies. Her optimistic personality continued to surface, blending into the character she was trying to create. In her music, however, that was exactly what she wanted to happen. Her goal was that her songs would reflect her feelings. She worked to make a personal statement with her second CD, *Hilary Duff*.

Hilary was excited about the music on her second CD. She said her songs were a better reflection of who she really was than her acting roles. She worked closely with the songwriters, talking to them about what was going on in her life. "It's very rock. Some of it's punky, but it's not too edgy," she said. "I just can't wait for people to hear it because they'll totally understand it and who I'm talking about and how I'm feeling inside." [52]

Hilary co-wrote two of the songs on the album, *Haters* and *Mr. James Dean*. *Mr. James Dean* referred to a girl recovering from a broken relationship who notes that her ex-boyfriend was nothing like the tough, cool Dean. Hilary also wrote *Haters* with her sister. Some people thought the song referred to her spats

Hilary felt that her second CD, Hilary Duff, *was more a reflection of who she was.*

with Lohan and Lavigne. Hilary said the song reflected the way that girls are mean to each other, an issue she had dealt with publicly. "I was reading about it along with millions of people," she said. "Most of it wasn't even true."[53]

Criticism and Cheers

The *Hilary Duff* CD was released in September 2004 on the Hollywood Records label and made it to No. 2 on the Billboard 200 chart. However, the album did not sell as well as *Metamorphosis*. It was criticized for Hilary's weak voice and the unoriginal songs. "The disc ultimately suffers from her unrelenting please-the-masses mission, with sweet but soulless vocals, cookie-cutter production and assembly-line songcraft on tunes such as the innocuous "Dangerous to Know" and the annoyingly sunny "Shine," wrote critic Chuck Arnold.[54]

The single "Fly" had a catchy chorus, and "I Am" was also strong, but the CD did not break new ground musically. Other critics agreed with Arnold. "The middle-school-poetry lyrics may strike a chord, but Duff's voice, a tiny thing that continues to lack a shred of musical personality, is buried under layers of generic cheese arrangements," said Ty Burr, a critic who gave the CD a grade D-.[55]

The Perfect Man

Hilary's next movie was also slated. While her films appealed to young girls, they did little to advance her acting ability or earn the respect of critics. *The Perfect Man,* which she made at the same time *Hilary Duff* was being recorded, was released in summer 2005. The lukewarm romantic comedy featured Hilary as Holly, a teen who was always moving around the country, thanks to her mother's obsession with finding the perfect man. Holly wanted to help her mom feel better about herself so she invented an admirer for her. When her mom, played by Heather Locklear, got interested in the guy, Holly had to find someone to fit the bill.

The movie's plot was criticized as too silly. It also lacked the humor it was supposed to have. "*The Perfect Man* takes its idiotic plot and uses it as the excuse for scenes of awesome stupidity,"

Heather Locklear played Hilary's mom in **The Perfect Man.**

noted critic Roger Ebert.[56] A scene in which Hilary's character sets off a sprinkler system in order to stop a wedding was one of those scenes, he said.

Dealing With Criticism

Hilary learned to take the criticism in stride. She knew she had put her best effort into her work and could not worry about what people said about it. "At first, when I got bad press and people would talk bad about my family or something like that, I would get really upset, but now it's just not worth my energy," she said. "I did get some bad reviews on the album—everybody does. People are going to say what they want to say and think what they want to think, and I can't change their minds."[57]

Hilary knew she had fans—she was selling millions of records and her concerts were sold-out. The audiences, mainly full of young girls and their parents, were not afraid to show they loved Hilary and her music. At a concert in California, the kids in the audience jumped up and down, singing the words to her songs. Hilary gave them a rock show with squealing guitars and crashing drums and they enjoyed it. "Duff was just as personable in concert as she is on TV and films," wrote reviewer Darryl Morden. "Sure, she's not a great singer, but she really does want to rock out. ... Duff's lightweight pop-rock isn't the stuff of grown-up music, but it's not supposed to be, and her best songs still have some hook appeal."[58]

Not Going it Alone

With all that she had going on—movies, music, and products to promote—Hilary needed some help to make sense of her life. One of the reasons she was so successful was the people she worked with. "I just have such a great team around me who knows how to schedule things so there isn't too much interference between all the things I'm working on," she said.

Carla Hay, "Hilary Duff: living a 'Cinderella' dream," *Billboard*, July 31, 2004, p. 12.

Even though critics were criticizing her singing and acting, Hilary continued to be popular in her concerts.

Growing the Right Way

There was no doubt Hilary was still popular with young girls. They bought her records, saw her movies, and cheered at her concerts. However, Hilary's ability as a performer was constantly questioned. Critics did not see anything outstanding about Hilary's voice or her acting ability.

Hilary faced a difficult time in her career. She continued to work and put a great deal of effort into her music and movies. However, critics had little respect for the work she was doing. She had to find a way to maintain her popularity and tackle more challenging projects at the same time.

Hanging in There

Hilary was growing up but still had a wholesome image that appealed to tweens. Their parents also liked her. They appreciated the fact that Hilary's music and movies were appropriate for their daughters. However, Hilary was not as appealing to kids her own age.

Hilary was now sixteen, and her peers did not always like things that had their parents' stamp of approval. It became more difficult for Hilary to release a record that matched the popularity of her first CD. Her acting also met with criticism, and she struggled to find a role that challenged her.

Work continued to be a constant factor in her life. Hilary considered movie offers, planned to do another album, and approved merchandise with her name on it. She needed to look beyond her daily schedule, however, if she was going to grow as an actress and as a singer. Hilary needed not only to look at what she had to do, she needed to think about where her career was going.

Confident But Criticized

In Hilary's favor was her strong self-image. She knew who she was: a teen who enjoyed her career and liked the fact that she was setting a good example for others. She did not worry about fitting in with the Hollywood party crowd. Instead, she looked to find a way to advance her career in a way that allowed her to keep her self-respect. Hilary admitted she had flaws, but she knew she was a hard worker with a positive image she wanted to protect. "I'm comfortable with who I am," she said. "I know where I'm going."[59]

Hilary's attitude and work ethic helped to keep her career going. Bob Cavallo, the chairman of the Buena Vista Music Group, was one of her biggest fans. He said her appeal was due to both her image and her willingness to work hard. "Sure, she's cute and wholesome," he said, "but she is also talented, intelligent, essentially decent and humble. You put those things together, along with incredible focus, and that really is something special."[60]

Not everyone was quite as taken with Hilary's wholesome image. Lohan and Lavigne continued to put down her talent. It seemed to Hilary that she was suddenly the butt of many jokes that made fun of her singing and her lifestyle. Hilary was hurt by their comments but tried to avoid spreading stories about others. She made no apologies for her wholesome image. She preferred to stay home rather than head out to parties, but noted "It's not like I stay home knitting, you know."[61]

Hilary also had to cope with negative reviews of her music and movies. This did not affect her career, however. Hilary wanted to continue to both sing and act. She put more of a rocking edge on her music and expected her sound to mature as she grew older. "Now my music is kind of pop-rock, right?" she said. "If I'm twenty-five and singing still, I don't want to be singing music like that."[62]

Romance with Joel

Hilary found an unlikely soulmate in her quest for a quiet lifestyle. In mid-2004 the sixteen-year-old began dating Joel Madden, a twenty-five-year-old singer and songwriter from the band Good Charlotte. They were seen together at restaurants and gatherings that summer and fall but did not admit that they were a couple until the following year.

At first glance, they looked like an unlikely pair. Madden was a tattooed rocker and she was a blonde who loved makeup. However, Hilary said that after two months together,

At first, Hilary and tattooed rocker Joel Madden looked like an unlikely pair.

she no longer noticed Madden's tattoos. She looked at the person he was inside, and he did the same with her. The main difference between them, Hilary said, was that she was stubborn and he was a pushover. Madden admitted to being a softie when it came to Hilary. "No one can push me around—except for her," he said.[63]

The couple shared the same morals, neither of them getting into the celebrity party lifestyle. They resisted staying out late and dancing on tables at clubs. Both were busy, shared an interest in music, and looked at the music business the same way. While Hilary was more optimistic and Madden tended to brood, Madden understood who she was beyond her image as a performer and actress, Hilary said. She was comfortable acting silly around him. She gained a sense of self-assurance by having him in her life. "He gave me a sense of confidence and independence I didn't have before," she said.[64]

Working for a Cause

Although Hilary had a busy schedule, she also found time to become involved with charitable organizations. She became part of Kids with a Cause, a nonprofit organization that helps children overcome poverty, hunger, sickness, and other issues. Hilary visited children in the hospital and also appeared at events for the organization.

In 2005, she announced that she would donate a portion of all ticket sales from her *Most Wanted* tour to help survivors of the earthquake and tsunami disaster in south Asia. She was also the youth ambassador for Return to Freedom, a wild-horse sanctuary. In addition, she did work for the Make-A-Wish-Foundation and the Armed Forces Foundation.

Collaboration

The pair managed to work their relationship around their busy schedules. While Hilary was on tour in Canada, Madden flew there to surprise her with dinner. Another time he flew to New York to meet her at the airport so they could fly back to Los Angeles together and have six hours to talk.

The pair worked together on Hilary's next album, *Most Wanted*. Madden co-wrote three songs on it and said he enjoyed working with his girlfriend. "It's fun," he said. "I'm really good at what I do. She's really good at what she does, so we do good things together."[65] Madden's brother Benji also helped with the album, and Benji was impressed by Hilary's work ethic. "I was like, 'Can we take a break? We've been singing for nine hours, girl!'"[66]

Most Wanted

Hilary's third album—*Most Wanted*—was released in August 2005. It was a collection of her hits and some new material.

Hilary went on tour with her third CD, Most Wanted, in 2005.

To promote her latest CD, Hilary appeared on **The Tonight Show with Jay Leno.**

The album's first single, "Wake Up," made it to No. 29 on the Billboard Top 40 chart and received positive reviews. "The song is generously doused with memorable lines and rhymes," said reviewer Chuck Taylor. "'Wake Up' will put her singing career on a par with her hyperactive acting endeavors."[67]

However, not every song met with an enthusiastic response. Reviewer Taylor was disappointed with "Beat of My Heart," saying it was a reminder of Hilary's days as a Disney Channel star. "Pop music is always appreciated, but this is a kiddie anthem," Taylor said, "plain and simple, so repetitive and childlike in its lyric ('the beat of my heart' is repeated 44 times in three minutes) that it is hardly a contender for contemporary radio."[68]

These comments did not slow Hilary down, however. She appeared on *The Tonight Show with Jay Leno, Today, Total Request Live,* and *Access Hollywood* to promote the album. Despite

Hil's Scent

While on her *Most Wanted* tour, Duff tested 115 fragrance variations before choosing one that would have her name on it. She wanted the perfume, called *With Love... Hilary Duff,* to reflect who she was and chose one with amber and Oriental scents.

Duff helped design the packaging as well. She used the colors painted on her bed, blue and purple, for the colors on the box. "I've always been drawn to fragrances that were a cross between something really sexy yet also very sweet," she said. "My own fragrance captures that."

People, September 4, 2006, p. 150.

Hilary's efforts, the album did not do as well as her previous releases. While *Most Wanted* hit No. 1 on the Billboard chart and sold 1.4 million copies, it was nowhere near the 3.9 million sold by *Metamorphosis.*

Mediocre Movies

Hilary also received disappointing reviews for her next two movies. She had a small role in *Cheaper by the Dozen 2,* the sequel to the comedy she had made with Steve Martin and an ensemble cast a few years earlier. She didn't seem to fit in with the laid-back cast, and although her role was meant to be more mature, she tended to be aloof.

Hilary next teamed up with her sister for the movie *Material Girls.* The movie was released in September 2006, and the two played a pair of rich sisters who were trying to save their father's cosmetics company. Reviewer Gregory Kirschling said the girls were "...so unsympathetic, exasperating, and smug from the get-go that you figure the movie has to be a send-up of the

Eating Habits

While working long days, Duff got into the habit of improving her mood and raising her energy level by eating M&Ms. When she was on a movie set, a few plain chocolate M&Ms revived her. She also developed a taste for junk food. Looking to live a healthier lifestyle, Duff changed her eating and exercise habits. She still ate desserts, but she watched how much she had. She took pizza and french fries out of her diet, and she did Pilates, a form of exercise, for strengthening. "You really start feeling stronger and better when you work out and eat healthier," she said.

Lori Berger, "Hilary Reinvented," *CosmoGirl*, May 2007, p. 130.

Hiltons, or the Olsens, or something," he said[69] and gave the film a grade of D-. Reviewer Elizabeth Weitzman of the *New York Daily News* noted that Hilary and Haylie could act and had chemistry, but he did not find anything good in the movie.

Hilary had been trying to look for roles that let her do something different with her acting career. This movie took it in the wrong direction, however. It was so bad that it earned Hilary and her sister a Razzie award nomination. The Razzies are given for the worst performances of the year.

Taking Care of Business

Despite a downturn in her album sales and poor movie reviews, Hilary's career did not stall. Although she was not doing as well with her music or acting as she had done earlier in her career, Hilary was still out there trying. And from a business standpoint she was doing better than ever—the magazine *Forbes* included her on its Celebrity 100 list in 2005.

Hilary may not have been the best singer or the most talented actress, but she always kept her fans in mind. Thinking about what people wanted helped her to continue selling products, CDs, and movies. Although her audience was not as large as it had been in the past, now was not the time for Hilary to make drastic changes. She continued to develop a clean image, one she felt comfortable with. Hilary realized that no matter how hard she worked, or how cleanly she lived her life, there would always be people who disapproved of what she did. Yet she remained true to her ideals. "I deal with a lot of negativity," she said. "People always take cheap shots at me. No matter what choices I make and as much as I give back, they take their shots."[70]

Hilary did not see herself competing directly with other teen pop stars. She was just working and doing the best she could. To Hilary, success was not a popularity contest. "It just seems like everybody's fighting over who can get their picture taken with who," she said. "Britney Spears, Jessica Simpson, Lindsay Lohan, me, everyone has their own thing going on. There's no need for jealousy."[71] As she approached eighteen, Hilary knew she had something to offer. She just had to figure out where she fit in.

Chapter 6

Maturing Image

ilary wanted to continue her career, but she needed to make some changes. She was growing up, maturing from a child star into a young adult. She had finished high school and was reaching the end of her teen years. She needed to find a way to develop a more mature image.

Hilary had been working like an adult since she was thirteen. After years in the entertainment industry, she felt more like a grown-up than a teen. She had managed to go from an ordinary child to a famous actress, singer, and businesswoman without falling into self-destructive habits. Now she faced the challenge of taking her career beyond her tween fans. Duff realized this would not be easy. Rather than relaxing and relying on the career she had built, Duff would need to keep working in order to keep her career from slipping.

New Look

To reach a broader audience, Duff made some changes. She hired a new manager and focused on music rather than movies. She also developed a new look, and went to fashion shows to see the latest trends. She fell in love with knee-high boots and big gold buckles. She began wearing more high heels, skinny jeans, and slinky tops.

It was not easy for Duff to grow out of her old image. She was only a few years removed from her Lizzie McGuire heyday, and the movies she made for Disney as a young teen continued to be shown on television. In many ways she still looked young. "With her honey-blond hair in a sideswept fringe and high, 1960s

As Hilary reached adulthood, she looked for ways to make her image more mature.

ponytail, Duff could almost be a Barbie brought to life," wrote writer Pauline O'Connor. "It's hard to think of another celebrity who so neatly embodies the wholesome, girl-next-door appeal that is the golden egg of the American tween market."[72]

However, Duff was making a subtle but noticeable statement that she was ready to grow up. When O'Connor met her, it was in a studio with pink tablecloths, pink lemonade, and pink T-shirts on the staff. Duff, however, wore all black. Although surrounded by a youthful atmosphere, she was breaking away from her girlishness. "I have to grow," she said. "I know I can do lots of other things. Now I wanna do things that free me."[73]

New Manager

Duff was ready to step out of her role as a tween queen and become a young woman. She described herself as driven and multifaceted. She knew, however, that running her career was not something she could do by herself. To make the most of her career, she brought in a new manager, Robert Thorne.

Thorne was an experienced manager who had been behind the Mary-Kate and Ashley Olsen movie and fashion empire for fifteen years. He had helped the twins turn their talent into a billion-dollar merchandising business. Thorne knew how to build a brand. He could help Duff develop a new image and build on her talent and popularity.

Thorne was impressed by Duff's fashion instincts and her ability to hold her own in business, film, and music. He wanted to make Duff's career a long one. "I have a craving to reach the next level," he said. "I'm passionate about establishing a brand that will stand decades in the market."[74]

Thorne began helping Duff to expand her career. She introduced a perfume that was produced by powerful cosmetics manufacturer Elizabeth Arden. Thorne predicted that her Web site, www.hilaryduff.com, would be the biggest Internet site for girls in the world. Publicity offices were opened in Canada and in other countries. To keep her younger fans happy, Duff introduced Barbie doll clothes and a doll with her image on it.

No matter what the age of her audience, Hilary gave them her best.

True to Her Fans

Although Duff wanted to develop a more mature image, there was no doubt that she remained popular with young fans. Duff did not intend to forget them. When she toured Canada in early 2006, playing at concerts in larger cities like Toronto and smaller ones like Moncton and Saint John, the kids in the audience were generally in the age range of seven to fourteen. Duff did not hold back on her performance at all. She treated the audience to a big production, bringing five musicians, three dancers, and two backup singers. She worked the stage so she came close to as much of the audience as possible.

The audience responded with ear-piercing screams. Duff's concert was impressive for its style and her ability to connect with the crowd. "As a vocalist, Duff is no Mariah Carey," wrote reviewer Alan Niester, of *The Globe and Mail,* "but she is certainly competent enough to deliver her pop songs with a polished air." He added that Duff pleased the audience with songs that offered more than light music and fluffy lyrics. "While songs such as the opening "Wake Up" and the later "Beat of My Heart" were frothy pop confections, many of her numbers ("Underneath My Smile," "Someone's Watching Over Me") were ballads with lyrical and emotional heft, relatively speaking,"[75] Niester wrote. Even when performing in front of a young audience, Duff's maturity was beginning to come through.

Independence

Duff also toured in Europe in 2006 and kept busy with promotions for her music, products, and perfume. As her career rolled along, her personal life hit a stumbling block. Duff broke up with Madden in late 2006.

Their split did not have anything to do with their age difference, Duff said, or anything that either had done. Rather, it was time for them both to move on. Duff ended their relationship when she did not feel it was right any more. "It wasn't like something was wrong," she said. "Breaking up was just something that I felt needed to happen between us."[76]

Their breakup led to rumors of another feud when Madden was spotted with Nicole Richie, who had starred with Paris Hilton in the television show *The Simple Life.* Although saddened by the end of the relationship, Duff insisted there were no bad feelings between the two. She admitted that it was difficult for her when Madden began dating Richie so soon after they broke up. She insisted, however, that they still had a good relationship and kept in touch through e-mail.

After ending their relationship, Duff took some time to enjoy her independence. She went out on dates but did not enter into any serious relationships. For now, she enjoyed being on her own. She wanted to just think about herself for awhile. Ending her relationship with Madden was sad and painful, but it gave her room to grow. "I'm not interested in being anybody's girlfriend," she said a few months after the breakup. "I'm interested in being a little selfish."[77]

Dignity

When Duff broke up with Madden, she was in the middle of working on a new CD, to be released in 2007. It was called *Dignity*. The CD's title reflected the way she tried to treat other people, her job, and even herself. And although Duff sometimes fell short of what she expected from herself, she tried to live her life in a way that she could be proud of.

For this CD, Duff co-wrote all but one track. She worked with songwriter Kara DioGuardi and said their songwriting sessions were like therapy. The songs were written as she was going through some difficult times in her personal life. She was breaking up with Madden, and her parents were also separating. Talking through the issues she faced helped Duff to deal with them. At first, Duff didn't want to address personal issues on the CD, but

Prickly Experience

When Duff made an appearance on the *Tyra Banks* show in 2007 to promote her *Dignity* CD, an animal encounter did not go quite as planned. Duff looked stunned when an animal trainer brought a porcupine onto the set. She was not as surprised as Banks, who climbed onto a chair to back away from the animal. Tyra tipped backwards on the chair and Duff ran over to help her up, as the porcupine sat quietly on the table.

then she decided that it was time to let people know that her life was not as ideal as it appeared to be. "Many of the songs are about things my family has gone through," she said. "I was scared to write about that stuff at first, but then I thought, why try to make it seem like I have a perfect life when I don't?"[78]

Duff put her heart into the CD but was sometimes frustrated that her songs did not receive more radio airplay. She thought this was because her sound was different from other popular bands. However, Duff was committed to producing an album that reflected her own sound. "She offers a balance between hip-hop and rock and she's already an iconic pop star crossing into a new generation, versus someone who simply has a nice song for radio," said record executive Abbey Konowich.[79]

Positive Reviews

Duff looked to reach more of a mainstream audience with her new album, and the early reviews were positive. She released the single "Play With Fire" in October 2006 and it reached No. 31 on the Hot Dance Club Play chart. Reviewer Chuck Taylor called the single innovative and was hopeful that Duff could bring a new sound to pop music. "'Play With Fire' is less of the clichéd little-girl-playing-tough-pop/rocker than it is a truly intriguing exploration into darker, more experimental melodic structures that could attract a whole new crowd of late-night dance floor minions to the Duff camp," Taylor wrote.[80]

While the CD had its share of dance music, some of the songs reflected a darker tone as they touched on the difficult times Duff was going through while the album was being made. Critic Jonathan Bernstein liked the result, giving the CD a B-plus grade and saying "She's never sounded less eager to please or more messily human... on the evidence of *Dignity*, heartache brings out the best in her."[81]

New Role

When Duff began making *Dignity*, she decided to put her acting career on hold for awhile. She did accept the opportunity to do voice work for the animated movie *Foodfight,* a film that looks at what happens in a grocery store after hours. The animated feature also included her sister, Haylie, in the cast. Although the nineteen-year-old was ready to try a character that was very different from the teens she'd been playing, Duff could find no interesting roles. She found that directors would not consider her for roles outside the ones she had been typically cast in. "It always shocks me the lack of openness, the lack of imagination that some casting directors have," Duff said. "I would read a script and be so in love with that, and someone would be like, 'Hilary Duff? Oh no, we don't want her for that.'"[82]

The mediocre reviews her movies had been getting also played a role in Duff's decision to concentrate more on her music. She wanted to try something far away from Lizzie McGuire, but at the same time she began doubting her acting skills. She put thoughts of acting behind her while she concentrated on writing and recording songs for *Dignity.*

A New Opportunity

While Duff was concentrating on her music, an unusual acting offer came up. Actor John Cusack had written a movie called *Brand Hauser: Stuff Happens.* The movie was later retitled *War, Inc.,* and Cusack cast himself in the title role. Cusack had written a part especially for Duff. She was contacted about the movie, but when she heard that Cusack wanted her to play a pop star she turned him down. That type of role was exactly what she did not want to be doing with her career.

However, Cusack persisted. He called Duff and explained that this pop star was nothing like Lizzie McGuire. The character was very mature and alluring and was from Eastern Europe. The independent movie would be an action film with a humorous edge. Cusack would play a hitman working for a company that wanted to earn profits from war. The film would also star his sister, Joan, and actress Marisa Tomei.

The part sounded interesting, and Duff agreed to make the movie. She went to Bulgaria where it was being filmed. Working

Mom, Come Home

At age nineteen, Duff began living on her own. Her mom moved out of the house they had shared and moved to another one that was five houses away. Hilary felt the need for some independence. "If I was leaving the house at night, my mom would say, 'You know you have to be somewhere early in the morning,'" she said, "and I'd be like, 'I *know*, Mom.'"

Although her mom was not living in the same house any more, Duff still asked that she come back on some nights. "The reality is that I need her," Duff said. "She's smart and tough, and there's still so much for me to learn from her."

Lori Berger, "Hilary Reinvented," *CosmoGirl*, May 2007, p. 128.

on the movie helped Duff regain her confidence as an actress. It showed her that she could reach inside herself to bring passion to her acting. "Before, I definitely considered myself more of a singer," she said. "I think definitely since I did the movie I was like, 'I'm an actress.'"[83]

Child Star No More

After making the movie, Duff's look changed as well. Her blond hair was replaced by long, dark curls for the role, and she liked the look so much that she kept it for awhile after filming ended. She also had a confident, edgy look and an upswept dark hairstyle on the cover of her *Dignity* CD.

The CD was one way that Duff proved she was growing up. She could not rely on what she had done as a young teen to drive a career as a young adult. As a young woman, she needed to reinvent herself and establish the next phase of her career. It was an emotional time for her as she dealt with her parents' divorce, her breakup with Madden, and the new direction in her career. However, she saw it as a time of growth. "It wasn't so much a conscious choice as it was a natural evolution," she said.[84]

Part of Duff's maturity included officially ending her feud with Lohan. In March 2007, they hung out together at a Hollywood club, chatting and dancing. "Whatever happened when we were young, it's over," Duff said. "She's really fun."[85]

Making Herself Happy

Duff remained popular with young girls and tweens but realized that to keep her career going, she needed to appeal to young adults as well. In her favor, she had a good attitude, a great work ethic, a respect for others, and a belief in herself. Duff was taking on projects that were new, different, and edgy, and looked to mature with her music as well. Duff was ready to take on the challenge of growing up.

Duff had been working since age eleven and had been going nonstop since she became Lizzie McGuire at age thirteen. She still considered herself to be a normal teen, however, even if her life was far from ordinary. Duff admitted that she missed out on

Continual Motion

Duff found Sundays to be her toughest day of the week. It was a day she was supposed to enjoy, but she found it difficult to sit back and do nothing. "I feel there's so much pressure for that day to be good," she said. "You're supposed to relax, and sometimes it makes you momentarily depressed and you don't know what to do with yourself. I'd much rather get to Monday."

Lori Berger, "Hilary Reinvented," *CosmoGirl*, May 2007, p. 128.

typical teen events by being a child star, but she also considered herself fortunate to have such a successful career. She knew she still had some growing to do—while she was still content with her good-girl image, she also wanted to remind people that she was now an adult. She was in charge of her life. "I've always been worried about what will make other people happy, and I'm trying to think more like, What's the best choice for myself?" she said.[86]

Different looks, songs, and types of movies were inevitable as Duff grew up. But Duff did not need to lose the good qualities that made her popular. She realized that her image was one of a nice, average teen. She now tried to balance that image with the message that she was maturing. Duff had something to say, and she did not want it to be overshadowed by an image that was outdated. "Change doesn't mean changing for the negative," she said. "For me, it's just growing as a person and an artist, and making sure I'm happy."[87]

Chapter 1: Fun, Frustration, and Lizzie McGuire

1. Walt Disney Records, "Hilary Duff Chat Transcript December 20, 2002," December 20, 2002, http://disney.go.com/disneyrecords/Song-Albums/santaclauslane/chat.html.
2. Taylor Hanson, "Hilary Duff," *Interview*, February 2004, p. 22.
3. *The Sunday Herald*, "On a Different Note," April 23, 2006, http://findarticles.com/p/articles/mi_qn4156/is_20060423/ai_n16229584.
4. Tim Carvell, "The Girl in the Bubble," *Entertainment Weekly*, May 9, 2003, p. 34.
5. Mark Dagostino, "Tween Queen," *People*, May 19, 2003, p. 83.
6. Laura Fries, "Lizzie McGuire," *Daily Variety*, January 17, 2001, p. 20.
7. *People*, "Teen Player," January 28, 2002, p. 71.
8. *People*, "Teen Player," January 28, 2002, p. 71.
9. Taylor Hanson, "Hilary Duff," *Interview*, February 2004, p. 122.

Chapter 2: Tween Queen

10. Lori Berger, "Teen Titans," *Teen People*, October 1, 2003, p. 120.
11. Alicia Clott, "What's Hilary Thinking?" *Girls' Life*, April/May 2002, p. 45.
12. Craig Rosen, "Hilary Duff: a performer's metamorphosis," *Billboard*, January 31, 2004, p. 10.
13. Craig Rosen, "Hilary Duff: a performer's metamorphosis," *Billboard*, January 31, 2004, p. 10.
14. Craig Rosen, "Hilary Duff: a performer's metamorphosis," *Billboard*, January 31, 2004, p. 10.
15. Alicia Clott, "What's Hilary Thinking?" *Girls' Life*, April/May 2002, p. 45.
16. David Nusair, "Six Disney Channel Original Movies," *Reel Film Reviews*, http://www.reelfilm.com/disorig.htm#cadet.

17. Leah Rozen, "Agent Cody Banks," *People,* March 24, 2003, p. 35.

18. Walt Disney Records, "Hilary Duff Chat Transcript December 20, 2002," December 20, 2002, http://disney.go.com/ disneyrecords/Song-Albums/santaclauslane/chat.html.

19. Adam Lambert, "The Lizzie McGuire Movie," *People,* May 12, 2003, p. 39.

20. David Noh, "The Lizzie McGuire Movie," *Film Journal International,* June 2003, p. 49.

21. Philip Kerr, "Roman tragedy," *New Statesman,* September 8, 2003, p. 46.

22. Alison Hope Weiner, "Lizzy Tizzy," *Entertainment Weekly,* June 13, 2003, p. 14.

Chapter 3: Metamorphosis

23. Bonnie Laufer-Krebs, "The Stuff on Hilary Duff," *Teen Tribute,* Fall 2003, p. 26.

24. Mark Binelli, "Teenager of the Year," *Rolling Stone,* September 18, 2003, p. 40.

25. Craig Rosen, "Hilary Duff: a performer's metamorphosis," *Billboard,* January 31, 2004, p. 10.

26. Craig Rosen, "Hilary Duff: a performer's metamorphosis," *Billboard,* January 31, 2004, p. 10.

27. Jon Caramanica, "Hilary Duff: Metamorphosis," *Rolling Stone,* September 18, 2003, p. 74.

28. Chuck Arnold, "Metamorphosis," *People,* September 8, 2003, p. 43.

29. Hilary Duff, "Teeny popper," *Texas Monthly,* April 2004, p. 80.

30. Hilary Duff, "Teeny popper," *Texas Monthly,* April 2004, p. 80.

31. Craig Rosen, "Platinum and Beyond," *Billboard,* January 31, 2004, p. 14.

32. Craig Rosen, "Hilary Duff: a performer's metamorphosis," *Billboard,* January 31, 2004, p. 10.

33. Kate Stroup, "Girl Power," *Newsweek,* March 17, 2003, p. 56.

34. Roger Ebert "Cheaper by the Dozen," *Chicago Sun-Times,* December 24, 2003, http://rogerebert. suntimes.com/apps/pbcs.dll/article?AID=/20031224/ REVIEWS/312240302/1023.

35. Bonnie Laufer-Krebs, "The Stuff on Hilary Duff," *Teen Tribute,* Fall 2003, p. 26.
36. Mark Binelli, "Teenager of the Year," *Rolling Stone,* September 18, 2003, p. 40.
37. Bonnie Laufer-Krebs, "The Stuff on Hilary Duff," *Teen Tribute,* Fall 2003, p. 26.
38. Tim Carvell, "The Girl in the Bubble," *Entertainment Weekly,* May 9, 2003, p. 34.
39. Taylor Hanson, "Hilary Duff," *Interview,* February 2004, p. 122.

Chapter 4: Ready for a Challenge

40. Taylor Hanson, "Hilary Duff," *Interview,* February 2004, p. 122.
41. "Hilary Duff Tries to Grow Up," *Entertainment Weekly,* August 1, 2003, p. 47.
42. Lisa Schwarzbaum, "A Cinderella Story," *Entertainment Weekly,* July 23, 2004, p. 55.
43. Quoted in Hilary Duff, Haylie Duff, "The Power Duff Girls," *People Weekly,* August 2, 2004, p. 77.
44. Chuck Arnold, "Hilary Duff: Hilary Duff," *People Weekly,* October 18, 2004, p. 43.
45. Donna Freydkin, "'Fessing up to celebrity feuding," *USA Today,* February 19, 2004, p. 2d.
46. Lori Berger, "Teen Titans," *Teen People,* October 1, 2003, p. 120.
47. Mark Binelli, "Teenager of the Year," *Rolling Stone,* September 18, 2003, p. 40.
48. Carla Hay, "Hilary Duff: Living a 'Cinderella' dream," *Billboard,* July 31, 2004, p. 12.
49. Quoted in Rosie Amodio, "Hangin' Out With Hilary," *Teen People,* November 1, 2004, p. 92.
50. Owen Gleiberman, "Raise Your Voice," *Entertainment Weekly,* October 15, 2004, p. 53.
51. *People,* "Raise Your Voice," October 18, 2004, p. 30.
52. Quoted in Rosie Amodio, "Hangin' Out With Hilary," *Teen People,* November 1, 2004, p. 92.

53. Jodi Bryson, "The very fortunate Hilary Duff," *Girls' Life,* August-September 2005, http://findarticles.com/p/articles/mi_m0IBX/is_1_12/ai_n15370450.

54. Chuck Arnold, "Hilary Duff: Hilary Duff," *People Weekly,* October 18, 2004, p. 43.

55. Ty Burr, "Hilary Duff," *Entertainment Weekly,* October 15, 2004, p. 72.

56. Roger Ebert, "The Perfect Man," *Chicago Sun-Times,* June 17, 2005, http://rogerebert.suntimes.com/apps/pbcs.dll/article?AID=/20050616/REVIEWS/50606003/1023.

57. Taylor Hanson, "Hilary Duff," *Interview,* February 2004, p. 122.

58. Darryl Morden, "Hilary Duff," *Hollywood Reporter,* September 7, 2004, p. 20.

Chapter 5: Hanging in There

59. Quoted in Rosie Amodio, "Hangin' Out With Hilary," *Teen People,* November 1, 2004, p. 92.

60. Nick Duerden, "The Golden Girl," *Blender,* October 2004, http://www.blender.com/guide/articles.aspx?id=1052.

61. Nick Duerden, "The Golden Girl," *Blender,* October 2004, http://www.blender.com/guide/articles.aspx?id=1052.

62. Taylor Hanson, "Hilary Duff," *Interview,* February 2004, p. 122.

63. Mark Dagostino, "The Princess and the Rocker," *People Weekly,* December 5, 2005, p. 141.

64. Lori Berger, "Hilary Reinvented," *CosmoGirl,* May 2007, p. 130.

65. Mark Dagostino, "The Princess and the Rocker," *People Weekly,* December 5, 2005, p. 141.

66. Quoted in Michelle Tauber, "Sweet 18," *People Weekly,* June 27, 2005, p. 130.

67. Chuck Taylor, "Hilary Duff: Wake Up," *Billboard,* July 16, 2005, p. 62.

68. Chuck Taylor, "Hilary Duff: Beat of My Heart," *Billboard,* November 26, 2005, p. 65.

69. Gregory Kirschling, "Material Girls," *Entertainment Weekly,* September 1, 2006, p. 53.

70. Jodi Bryson, "The very fortunate Hilary Duff," *Girls' Life,* August-September 2005, http://findarticles.com/p/articles/mi_m0IBX/is_1_12/ai_n15370450.

71. Quoted in Michelle Tauber, "Sweet 18," *People Weekly,* June 27, 2005, p. 130.

Chapter 6: Maturing Image

72. Pauline O'Connor, "I'm with the brand," *The Sunday Times,* November 12, 2006, p. 15.

73. Quoted in Pauline O'Connor, "I'm with the brand," *The Sunday Times,* November 12, 2006, p. 15.

74. Quoted in Pauline O'Connor, "I'm with the brand," *The Sunday Times,* November 12, 2006, p. 15.

75. Alan Niester, "Scream! Duffster gives it her all," *The Globe and Mail,* January 24, 2006, p. R3.

76. Quoted in Lori Berger, "Hilary Reinvented," *CosmoGirl,* May 2007, p. 128.

77. Quoted in Lori Berger, "Hilary Reinvented," *CosmoGirl,* May 2007, p. 128.

78. Quoted in Lori Berger, "Hilary Reinvented," *CosmoGirl,* May 2007, p. 128.

79. Chuck Taylor, "Duff Gets Personal on Dance-Driven Album," *Billboard* http://www.billboard.com/bbcom/feature/article_display.jsp?vnu_content_id=1003562257.

80. Chuck Taylor, "Play With Fire," *Billboard,* November 25, 2006, p. 52.

81. Jonathan Bernstein, "Duff in a Huff," *Entertainment Weekly,* April 6, 2007, p. 75.

82. Nekesa Mumbi Moody, "Balancing Act," *The Courier Mail,* May 3, 2007.

83. Nekesa Mumbi Moody, "Balancing Act," *The Courier Mail,* May 3, 2007.

84. Lori Berger, "Hilary Reinvented," *CosmoGirl,* May 2007, p. 128.

85. Molly Lopez, et al, "Insider," *People,* April 16, 2007, p. 63.

86. Lori Berger, "Hilary Reinvented," *CosmoGirl,* May 2007, p. 128.

87. Lori Berger, "Hilary Reinvented," *CosmoGirl,* May 2007, p. 128.

1987

Hilary Duff is born in Houston, Texas.

1993

Hilary and Haylie begin trying out for roles in commercials and are successful in getting parts.

1996

Hilary, Haylie, and their mother, Susan, move to California.

1998

Hilary gets the starring role in the movie *Casper Meets Wendy*.

2000

After trying out four times, Hilary gets the lead role in the television series *Lizzie McGuire*.

2001

Lizzie McGuire premiers in January to positive reviews. It is soon a favorite among young teens and preteens.

2002

Hilary gets a lead role in the Disney movie *Cadet Kelly* and releases the Christmas album *Santa Claus Lane*.

2003

Lizzie McGuire moves from television to the theater with *The Lizzie McGuire Movie*. Hilary also gets a small role in *Cheaper by the Dozen*. She leaves Lizzie McGuire behind and the series ends after sixty-five episodes. She releases the CD *Metamorphosis*.

2004

In addition to releasing the CD *Hilary Duff*, she makes the feature films *A Cinderella Story* and *Raise Your Voice*.

2005

The album *Most Wanted* is released, and Duff makes the movies *Cheaper by the Dozen 2* and *Material Girls*.

2007

The album *Dignity* is released in April. Duff appears in the movies *Foodfight!* and *War, Inc.* and makes the film *Talking with Dog*.

Books

Marylou Morano Kjelle, *Hilary Duff*. Hockessin, Delaware: Mitchell Lane Publishers, 2005. A brief, easy-to-read account of Duff's life.

Nancy Krulik, *Hilary Duff: A Not-so-typical Teen*. New York: Simon Spotlight, 2003. A biography of Duff, including a list of her movies and albums.

Matthew Rettenmund, *Hilary Duff: All Access*. New York, Berkley Boulevard Books, 2005. A behind-the-scenes look at Duff's career.

Web Sites

Hilary Duff (www.hilaryduff.com). The star's official Web site, with information about her music, movies and products. There's also a blog and a fan club link.

Internet Movie Database (www.imdb.com). Search for Hilary Duff to find a list of the actress's movie credits, as well as a photo gallery.

MTV (www.mtv.com). Search for Hilary Duff to find her music videos and articles about the star.

TV.com (www.tv.com). To see a list of *Lizzie McGuire* episodes, search for the show.

Index

Picture Credits

Terri Dougherty is a reporter and writer who enjoys writing books for children and young adults. She lives in Appleton, Wisconsin, with her husband, Denis, and their three children, Kyle, Rachel, and Emily. When she's not writing, she enjoys traveling with her family, going to her kids' sporting events, and playing soccer. Staying up late to watch *A Cinderella Story* with her youngest daughter is also not a bad way to spend an evening.